The Usborne Nature Trail Book of
BIRDWATCHING

Written by Malcolm Hart and Margaret Stephens
Series Editor Sue Jacquemier
Consultant Editor Peter Holden, National Organizer of the Young Ornithologists' Club
Assistant Editor Jane Stephenson
Editorial revision by Margaret Stephens
Designed by Mike Ricketts
Design revision by Amanda Barlow

Illustrated by
Mike Atkinson, Gillian Platt, Graham Austin, Andrew Beckett, Roger Kent (The Garden Studio), Dave Ashby, Isabelle Bowring, Hilary Burn, Colin King, Ken Lilly, Richard Millington, Charles Pearson, Maurice Pledger.

If you are walking along a seashore, rambling in the countryside or sitting in a city garden, you can alway[s] find birds. This book will help you to identify them and give you lots of information about their habits.

When you go bird spotting take this book with you and turn to the pages which deal with the kind of place you are visiting, such as a wood or pond. The pages at the back of the book will give you extra help by showing you the size of certain birds.

If you have enjoyed learning about birds in this book, then on the last page there is a list of clubs and books to help you go further.

Bluetit

Nuthatch

The birds on these pages are not drawn to scale

The Usborne Nature Trail Book of BIRDWATCHING

Contents

Siskin

First published in 1976 by
Usborne Publishing Ltd
83-85 Saffron Hill
London EC1N 8RT, England
Revised 1992.

Printed in Belgium

How to be a birdwatcher

The most important thing to have when you go birdwatching is a notebook. If you try and keep all the facts in your head, you will probably forget some of the important ones.

Make sure any notes you make are clear and readable. The picture on the right shows how to set your notebook out. Try to draw the birds you see. Even a bad drawing is better than no drawing at all.

If you can, take this book with you on bird spotting trips. It will help you to identify the birds you see.

Look carefully for the shape and obvious marks first. The male Reed Bunting here has a sparrow-like body and beak, a dark head, white collar and white outer tail feathers. It also has a dark throat and dark flecks on its side.

Male Reed Bunting

A birdwatcher has to take notes quickly. Use a spiralbound notebook, like the one here. It has a stiff back to help you write easily. File your notes away in date order when you get home or write them up into a neat book. When you are out, put your notebook in a plastic bag to keep it dry.

Black head
White collar
2nd August 1991
Weather - Sunny
Clare Park
M Reed Bunting
Dark Brown streaked back
Grey-white underneath
Flight Pattern
Also F carrying grass (for * ?)

Make sure you have all the details of place, date, time of day and weather entered in your notebook.

Bird shorthand

M = MALE
F = FEMALE
JUV = JUVENILE (YOUNG BIRD NOT IN ADULT FEATHERS)
* = NEST
C10 = ABOUT TEN (WHEN TALKING ABOUT NUMBERS OF BIRDS)

Use these signs instead of writing out the words. It will save you time. Always take two pens or pencils with you.

How to stalk birds

In the countryside there is plenty of opportunity to see many types of birds. When you go birdwatching camouflage your shape by standing in front of or behind a tree or bush. Keep the sun behind you, so you are in shadow. If there is no cover, crawl closer using your elbows and feet. Don't wear clothes that rustle when you move. Never move quickly in the open.

Willow Warbler

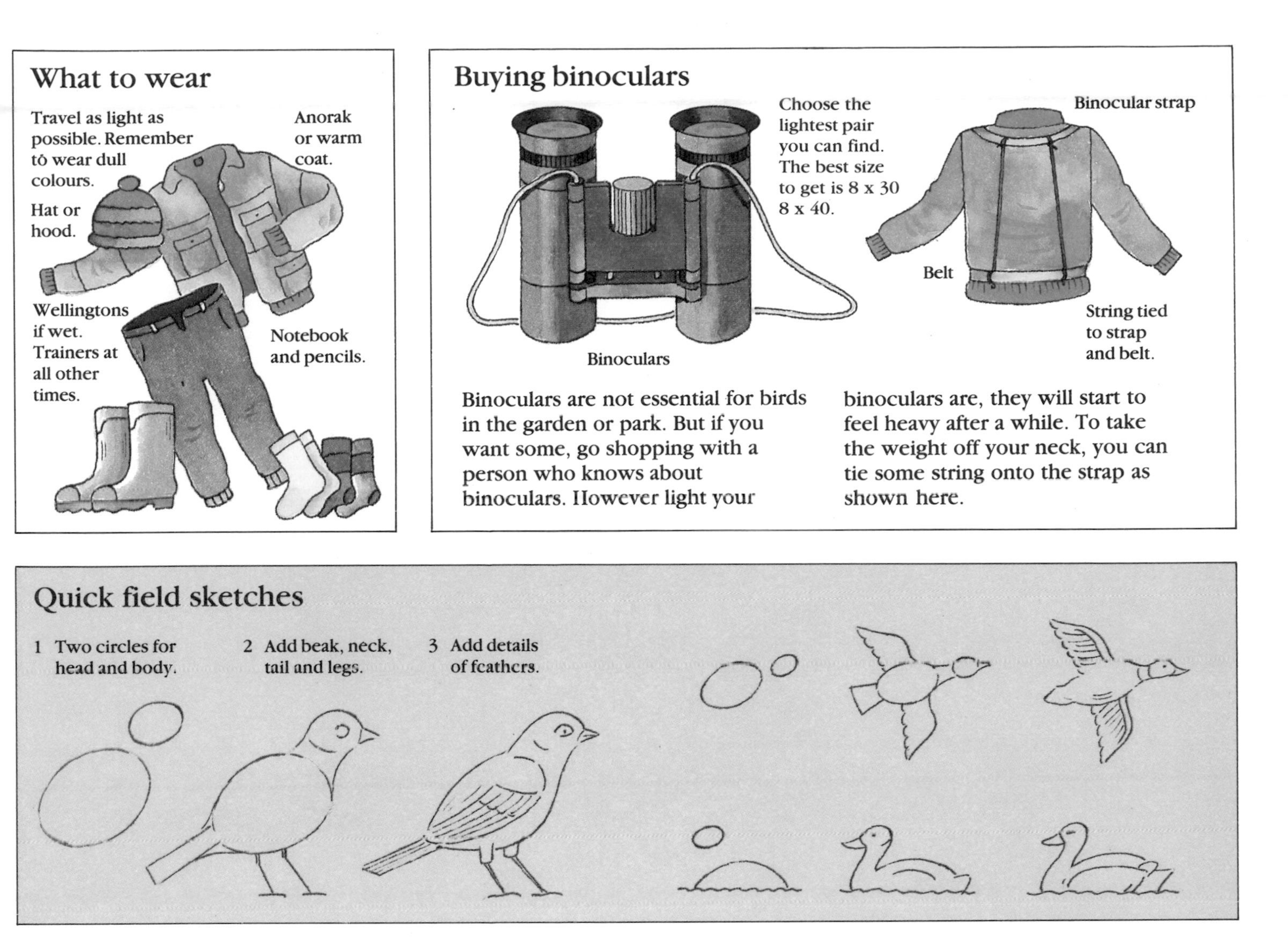

What to wear

Travel as light as possible. Remember tô wear dull colours.

Buying binoculars

Choose the lightest pair you can find. The best size to get is 8 x 30 8 x 40.

Binoculars are not essential for birds in the garden or park. But if you want some, go shopping with a person who knows about binoculars. However light your binoculars are, they will start to feel heavy after a while. To take the weight off your neck, you can tie some string onto the strap as shown here.

Quick field sketches

The best way to make notes on the birds you see is to draw quick sketches of them. Begin by drawing two circles - one for the body and one for the head. Notice the size and position of the head and body before you start. Add the tail, beak, legs and then add details of feathers if you have time. Do not draw what you do not see. Practise by drawing the birds you can see from your window or sit on a bench in the park and draw the birds there.

Remember to use your ears as well as your eyes. Birdsong is very important when you go birdwatching. It is often the first clue to tell you that a bird is near. The Jay, pictured here, has a very raucous call . Other sounds can give you clues too. You will often hear a Green Woodpecker drilling a hole in a tree before you see it.

You will not get far loaded with heavy equipment and you will be unable to move easily and quietly. If birds can see your shape silhouetted against the sky, they will fly off.

Chaffinch

Nuthatch

Jay

Chaffinch

What to look for

These pages tell you what to look for when you want to identify a bird.

When you see a bird for the first time, there are several questions you should ask. What size is it? Has it any obvious marks, such as the Reed Bunting's black head and white outer tail feathers? How does it fly and feed? How does it behave? Where is it? What colour is it?

Sometimes differences in colour can be confusing. There are some examples of this on the page opposite.

This is a female Sparrowhawk chasing a male Reed Bunting. The labels give examples of the kind of thing to note down when you see a bird.

Flight patterns

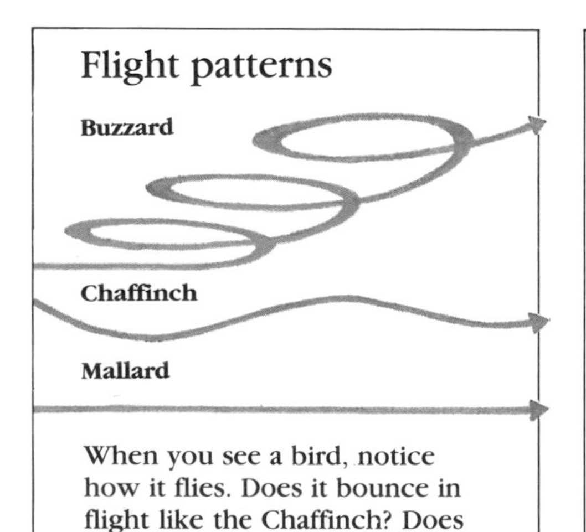

When you see a bird, notice how it flies. Does it bounce in flight like the Chaffinch? Does it float and soar like the Buzzard, or fly fast and straight like a Mallard?

Shapes in flight

Crow
Heron
Goose
Tern
Curlew
Magpie
Woodpecker

What sort of shapes does a bird make when it is flying? Are the neck and tail long or short?

Has it got short rounded wings or long narrow ones? Do its feet stick out behind its tail?

Sex differences

The males of some birds, such as the Blackbird, have different coloured feathers and beaks from the females.

Colour changes

Some birds, such as the Black-headed Gull, have a different plumage in winter from the plumage they have in summer.

Age differences

In some birds, such as the Robin, the young look very different from their parents.

Looking at beaks

Beaks can give you clues to what a bird eats. The Carrion Crow's beak is an all-purpose tool. The Greenfinch's beak is more suited to eating seeds.

The Curlew uses its long beak to probe for food in mud. The Grey Heron's beak is even longer and is used to catch fish, frogs and insects.

One way to identify a bird is from its song. Go out with someone who knows birdsong well, or borrow records of birdsong from your library

Watch what birds are doing

The Grey Wagtail often patrols in mud or short grass. It wags its tail up and down. Sometimes it makes a dash after an insect.

The Treecreeper creeps up the trunk of a tree, picking out insects from cracks in the bark with its thin, curved bill.

The Turnstone walks along the beach turning over seaweed and stones, looking for small creatures, such as shellfish, to eat.

Clues and tracks

Sometimes you may not be able to see all the birds that live in an area. Even if you don't see them, special clues can tell you they are present. Some of these clues are easy to spot, such as feathers and the remains of meals.

You may not be able to identify the feathers you find straight away. But later you may see a dead bird, or a bird in a book, that has feathers like the ones you have collected. Remember that most birds have feathers of many different sizes and colours.

Jay feather

Sandwich Tern egg eaten by a **gull.**

Magpie feather

Oystercatcher skull

Jackdaw pellet

Sparrowhawk pellet

Curlew feather

Always make sure you have something to keep the objects in that you collect. Label everything carefully with lots of detail - the more information the better. Always wash your hands after touching things you have collected.

Pine cone nibbled by a **squirrel.**

Hazelnut pecked at by a **Great Tit.**

Hazelnut pecked at by a **Woodpecker.**

When you find the remains of nuts and pinecones that have been nibbled, remember that it may not have been a bird. Squirrels and mice eat these as well. So, be careful when you identify the nibbler.

Collecting feathers and wings

Cuts

Sticky tape

Quill

Date

Where found

Bird

Type of feather

Pin

Pin

Pin

Fix the feathers you find in an exercize book, as shown here, and write notes beside them. Make two cuts, 6 mm apart, in the page. Thread the feather through and then stick the quill down with sticky tape.

Wings cut from dead birds can be dried and kept. Pin the wing out on a piece of stiff board. It should dry in a few days and can then be placed in an envelope with a label and some mothballs.

Pinecones

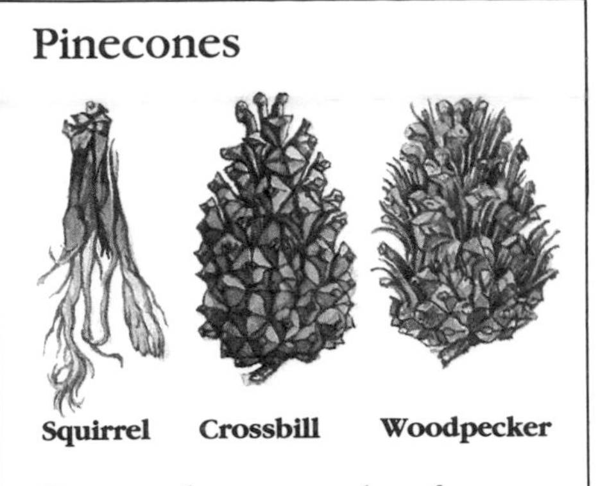

Here are three examples of pinecones that have been nibbled by birds or animals. They break open the cones in different ways as they search for seeds to eat.

Nuts

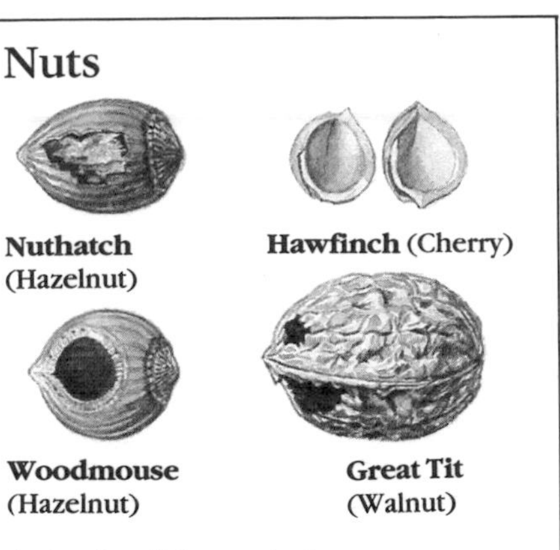

Animals all have their own ways of opening nuts. Mice chew neat little holes, while some birds leave jagged holes and others split the nuts in half.

The Song Thrush's anvil

Song Thrushes use a stone like an anvil to break open snail shells. Look for the anvil - it will be surrounded by the remains of the bird's meal.

Owl pellets

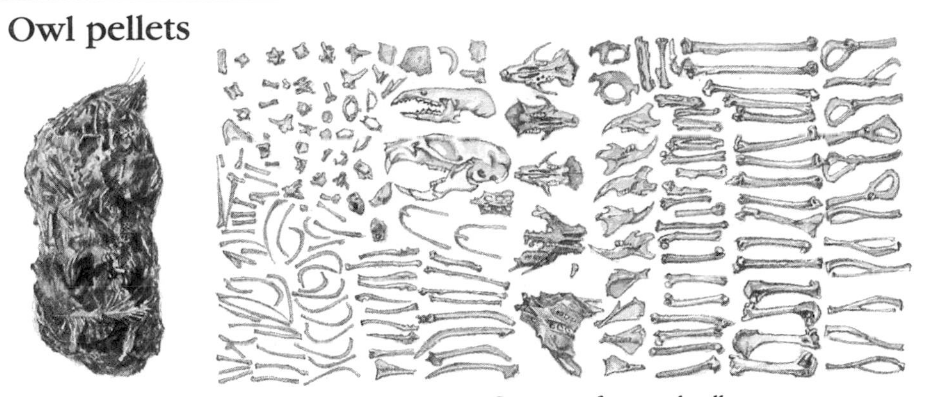

Contents of one owl pellet.

Owls swallow small animals and birds whole, and then cough up the fur, feathers and bones as a pellet. You can find these beneath trees or posts where the owl rests. Pull a pellet apart and sort out the bones. The easiest bones to identify are the skulls of animals the owl has eaten.

Other pellets

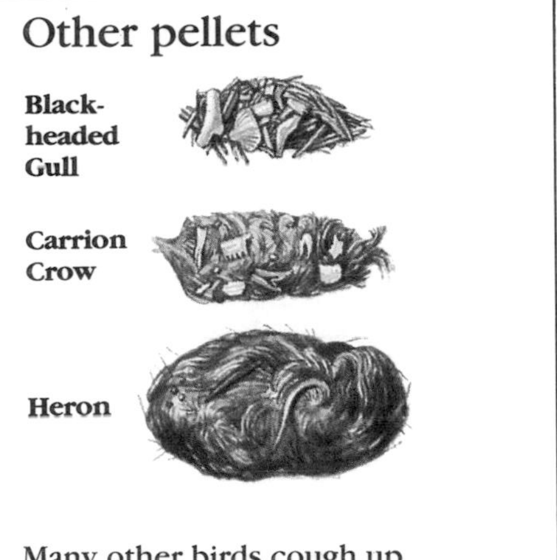

Many other birds cough up pellets. But it is harder to identify what is inside them, as most birds do not eat large animals.

Footprint casts

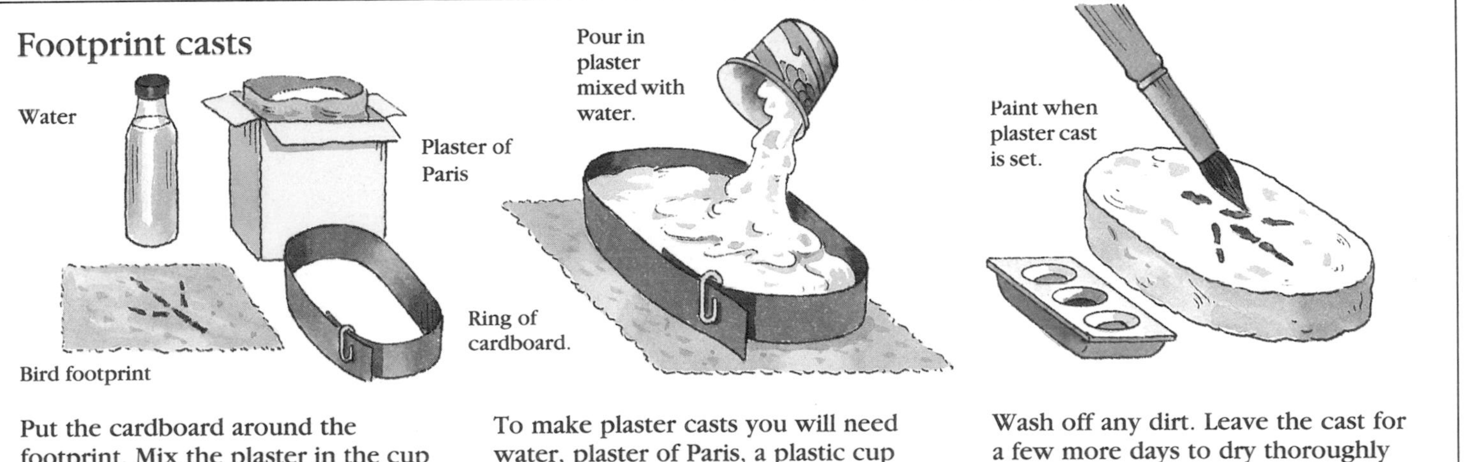

Put the cardboard around the footprint. Mix the plaster in the cup and pour it into the ring. Let it harden for 15 minutes. Take the cast and its cardboard home.

To make plaster casts you will need water, plaster of Paris, a plastic cup or glass and a strip of cardboard bent into a ring, and fastened with a paperclip.

Wash off any dirt. Leave the cast for a few more days to dry thoroughly and then carefully remove it from the cardboard. Paint the footprint and then varnish it.

Making a bird garden

On these pages you can see many of the birds that visit gardens or window sills for food. Different kinds of food attract different birds. Put out bones, suet, cheese, oats, peanuts, currants and bits of bacon rind. Scatter some food in the open though for birds that prefer to eat on the ground. A good way of attracting birds is by building a bird bath and a bird table for your garden.

Putting out food

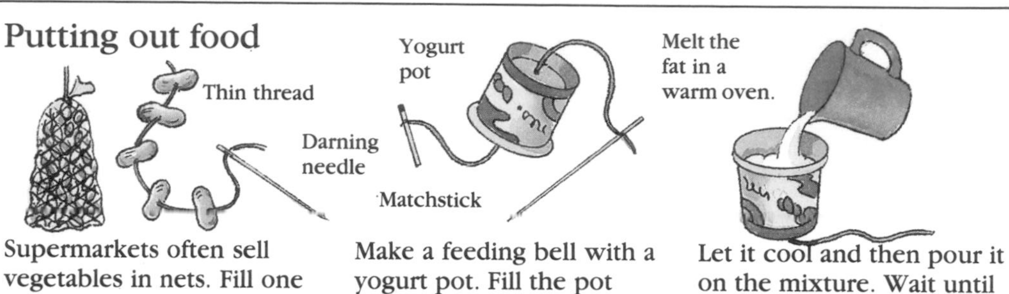

Supermarkets often sell vegetables in nets. Fill one of these with unsalted peanuts, or thread peanuts in their shells on thread or thin string, and hang them up in the garden.

Make a feeding bell with a yogurt pot. Fill the pot with breadcrumbs, currants, cooked potato and oatmeal. Ask an adult to help you melt some fat.

Let it cool and then pour it on the mixture. Wait until it hardens and then pull some thread through it as shown in the picture. Hang it upside down with the thread.

Make a bird table

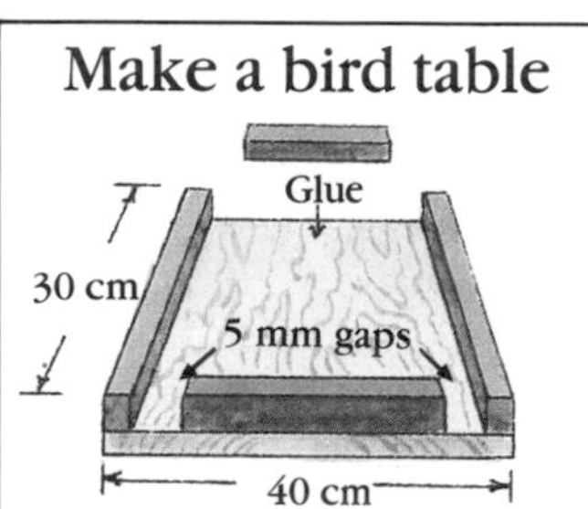

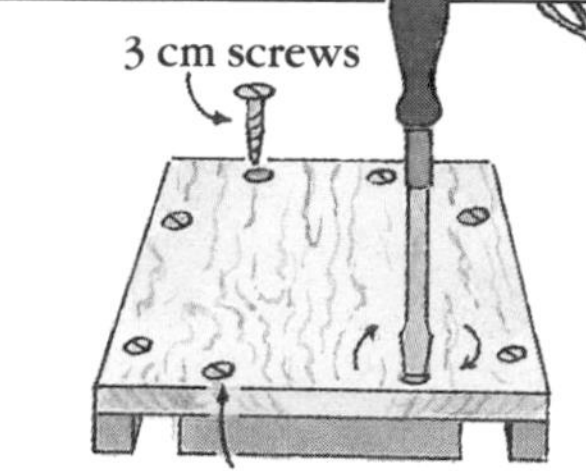

Put screws in under batten strips.

Gaps let rain water drain off.

You will need a piece of outdoor quality plywood about 40 cm x 30 cm and four strips of batten about 30 cm long. Glue the battens to the plywood as shown above.

When the glue has dried, turn the table over and put in two screws on every side, as shown above. Protect your table with a wood preservative and screw it to a wooden box.

To make a hanging table, put four screw-eyes into the sides and use string to hang it from a branch, as shown above. Clean the table regularly with disinfectant.

Make a bird bath

Make sure the polythene has no holes.

Choose a place not too close to the feeding area you have set up. Dig a hole with sloping sides, about 15 cm deep and 1 m wide. Dig from the middle out.

Line the hole with strong polythene (a dustbin liner will do). Weight the polythene down with stones and sprinkle gravel or sand over the lining.

Put a few stones and a short branch in the middle to make a perch. Fill the bath with water. Keep it full and make sure it is free from ice in winter.

Feeding chart

Make a chart of the kinds of food you see different birds eating. Which birds like nuts best? Tick the boxes each time you see a bird eat something.

Soon you will know which foods are popular and can make sure they are always in the garden.

Key to birds

1 Greenfinch
2 House Sparrow
3 Blue Tit
4 Robin
5 Coal Tit
6 Starling
7 Chaffinch
8 Blackbird
9 Mistle Thrush
10 Goldfinch
11 Song Thrush
12 Dunnock
13 Bullfinch

7

8 Femal

10

10

Plants that birds like to eat

All these plants are good bird food. If you have a garden, try to let a little patch grow wild. Weeds, such as Groundsel, have seeds that birds like to eat. Trees and bushes, such as Rowan, have lots of good berries in the autumn. Some birds like over-ripe apples and sultanas. Dig over a patch of earth, so you make it easier for some birds to find worms and insects.

Making a nesting box

Encourage birds to visit your garden in spring by building a nesting box. If the entrance hole is small then a Blue Tit will probably nest there. If the hole is larger then you may find a House Sparrow using it.

Other birds, such as Great Tits, Starlings, Tree Sparrows and Wrens, sometimes use nesting boxes. Try not to go close up to the box if birds are nesting there, as you will frighten them away. You can always watch them from indoors.

Side removed to show how box is made.

To make your nesting box you will need some plywood that is 12 mm thick with an overall length of 900 mm and width of 254 mm.

How to cut the wood

A Back

B Front

C Base

Waste

241 D Side 102 254

254 E Side 102 241

Top F

G

H

Waste

J Main support

Battens

First cut the pieces in these sizes

- A 254 mm x 127 mm
- B 241 mm x 127 mm
- C 127 mm x 127 mm
- D See diagram
- E See diagram
- F 152 mm x 127 mm
- G 102 mm x 25 mm
- H 102 mm x 25 mm
- J 510 mm x 25 mm

Drill the entrance hole with a hand drill about 50 mm from the top of the front section. The hole should be 25 mm wide.

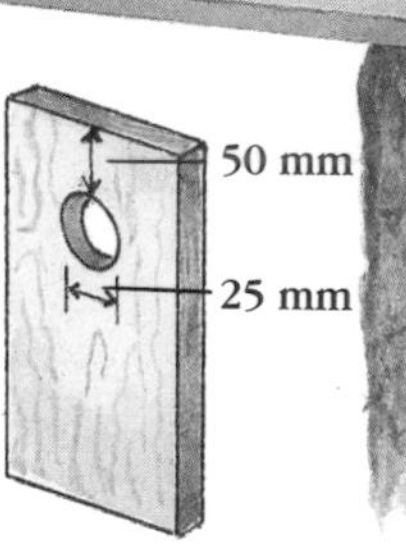

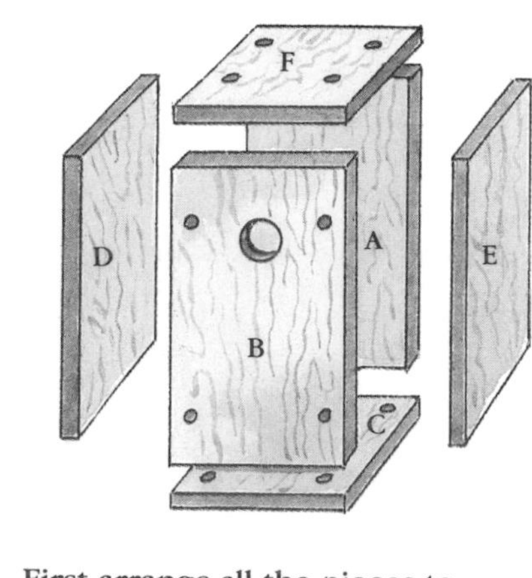

First arrange all the pieces to make sure that they fit together properly. Then drill holes for all the screws.

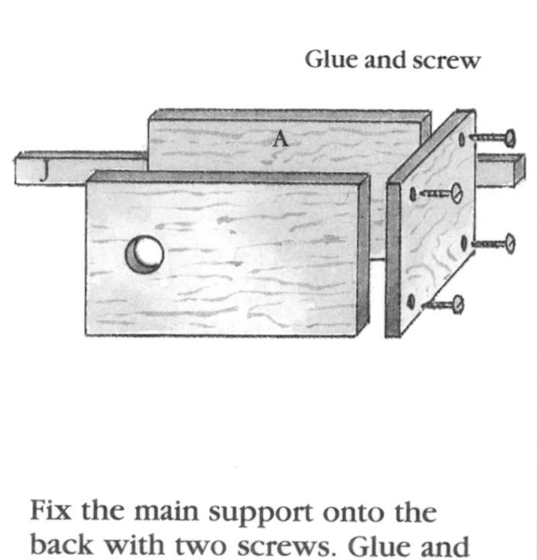

Fix the main support onto the back with two screws. Glue and screw the bottom onto the back and then the front.

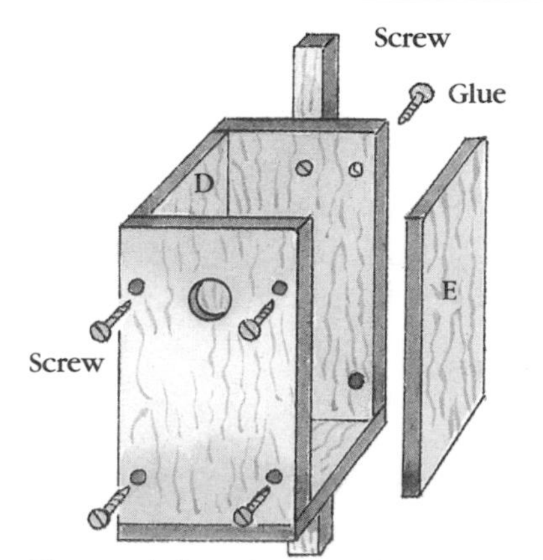

Glue and then fit the side pieces into place. Screw them on if they fit properly. If they don't, check the measurements carefully.

Where to put the box

Your completed nesting box should be fixed to a tree trunk or to a wall that is covered with a climbing plant, such as ivy. If there is no climbing plant, a bare wall or tree trunk will do. The entrance hole should not face south or west as the heat from direct sunlight might kill the young birds. Fix it about 2 m or more above the ground, well away from cats. Every winter, take it down and empty out the old nest. Disinfect the box and give it a new coat of wood preservative before replacing it.

Side removed to show how box is made.

Other types of box

Special nesting boxes can be bought for House Martins. You can fix them under the edge of the roof.

An open-fronted box is good for other birds. Make it like the first box, but cut an opening as shown in the picture above.

Keeping a record

Try to make a note of what happens in your nesting box. If a bird nests in the box there will be many details to record throughout the spring and summer.

You may even see some birds visiting the box in winter. They use boxes to sleep in. The notes below tell you the sort of thing to record.

1 Date of first visit.
2 Number of birds visiting.
3 Date bird first enters box.
4 Date birds bring nest material.
5 Type of nest material.
6 Date birds first bring food.
7 Type of food.
8 Date young leave nest.

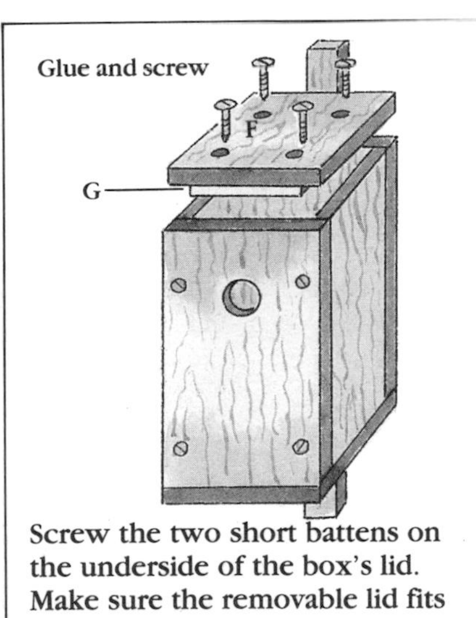

Screw the two short battens on the underside of the box's lid. Make sure the removable lid fits tightly and securely.

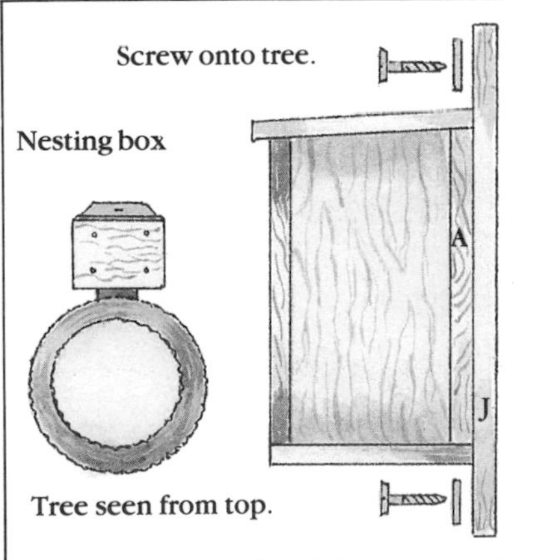

Paint the outside of the box with wood preservative and let it dry. Screw or nail it on to a tree (see above).

The nesting season

The nesting season is a time of great activity for all birds. First they must find a mate and then start looking for a place to build a nest and feed. The spot they choose becomes their territory. Next they lay their eggs and rear their young.

With all this going on it is not difficult to find out where some birds are building a nest or feeding their young. A bird carrying something in its beak, such as worms or grass, is the most common sign. On these pages you will find some more clues to help you.

A parent Song Thrush arrives at the nest. The young birds beg for food with wide open mouths. The parent puts food into their mouths and then flies off on another food-hunting expedition.

Food chart

Make a food chart to record which birds you see carrying food to their young, and record the type of food.

FOOD CHART

	WORMS	SNAILS	INSECTS
BLACK-BIRD			
ROBIN			
SONG THRUSH			

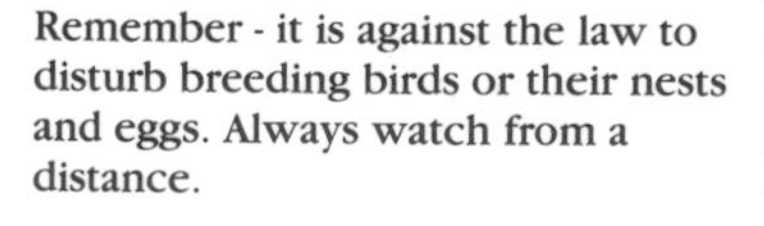

Remember - it is against the law to disturb breeding birds or their nests and eggs. Always watch from a distance.

Spotting nesting birds

Rook

In the spring, you will often see birds carrying nest material in their beaks. Rooks break off large twigs to make their nests.

Nightingale

Look out and listen for a bird singing in the same place every day during spring and summer, such as the Nightingale. It is probably breeding.

Stonechat

You may see adult birds carrying droppings away from the nest in their beaks. They do this to keep the nest clean for their young.

Nest materials

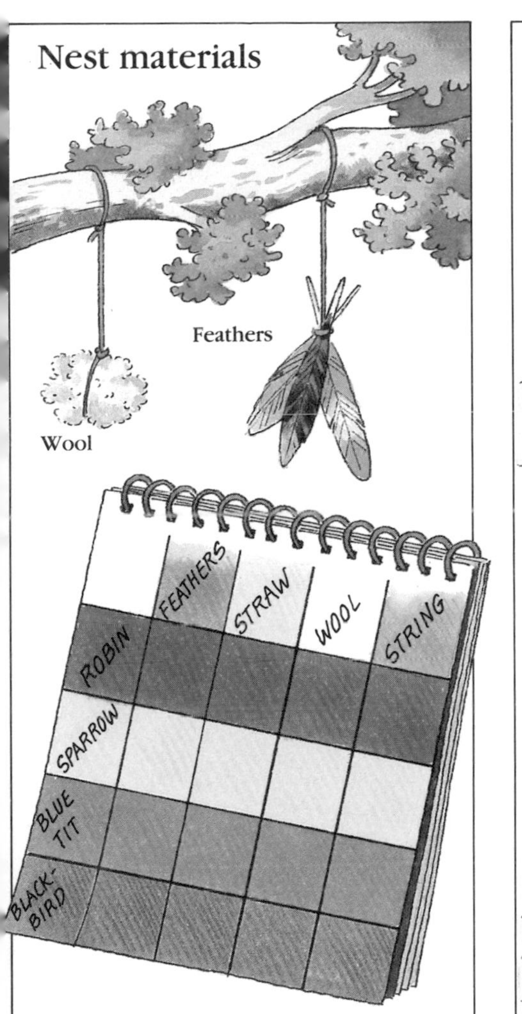

Hang up bits of wool, feathers, straw and string from a tree. Make a note of what different materials birds collect to use for their nests.

Where birds nest

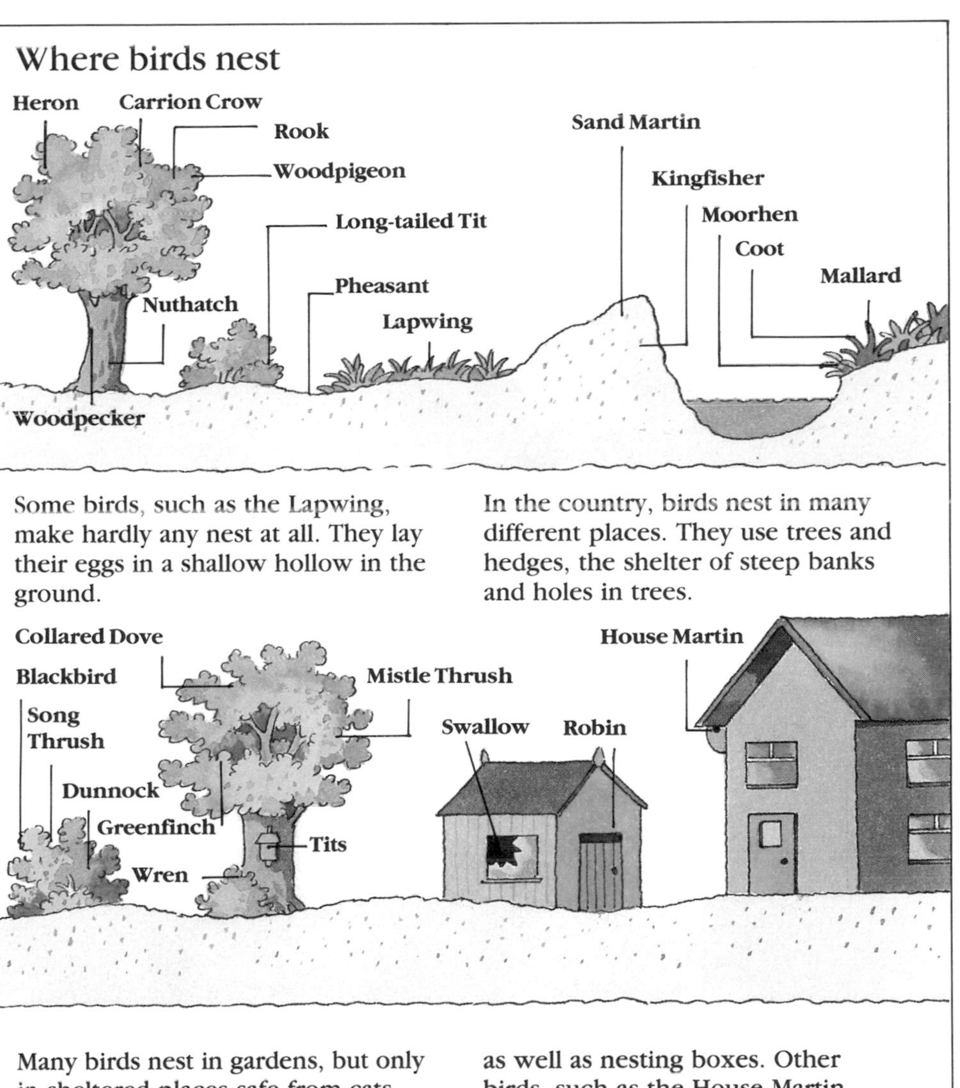

Some birds, such as the Lapwing, make hardly any nest at all. They lay their eggs in a shallow hollow in the ground.

In the country, birds nest in many different places. They use trees and hedges, the shelter of steep banks and holes in trees.

Many birds nest in gardens, but only in sheltered places safe from cats and dogs. They use thick bushes, trees, ivy-covered walls and sheds, as well as nesting boxes. Other birds, such as the House Martin, build under the roof, and Barn Owls can nest on a ledge in an old barn.

Ponds and inland waterways

Ducks are the birds you are most likely to see on a pond. They have quite long necks, webbed feet and wide, flat bills. They are all good swimmers. Most ducks feed on water plants in the pond.

Ducks can be divided into three kinds. There are diving ducks, such as the Tufted Duck, and dabblers, such as the Mallard. The most rare are the fish-eating ducks called sawbills.

In spring and summer, you will often see ducklings trailing behind their parents on the water's surface, or even hitching a piggy-back ride.

Webbed feet are best for swimming. The web opens to push hard against the water. When the foot comes back. the web closes so that the foot does not drag through the water.

Coots and Moorhens spend more time on land. Coots' feet are partly webbed. Moorhens have hardly any webbing. Their heads jerk backwards and forwards when the birds swim.

New ducklings are taken to the water by their mother. The ducklings fall in and can swim straight away.

Male and female Mallards have a blue flash on each wing called a speculum.

Great Crested Grebes are fish eaters. The male and female both look after their chicks, carrying them on their backs.

Long, flat bills are useful to sift food.

How water birds feed

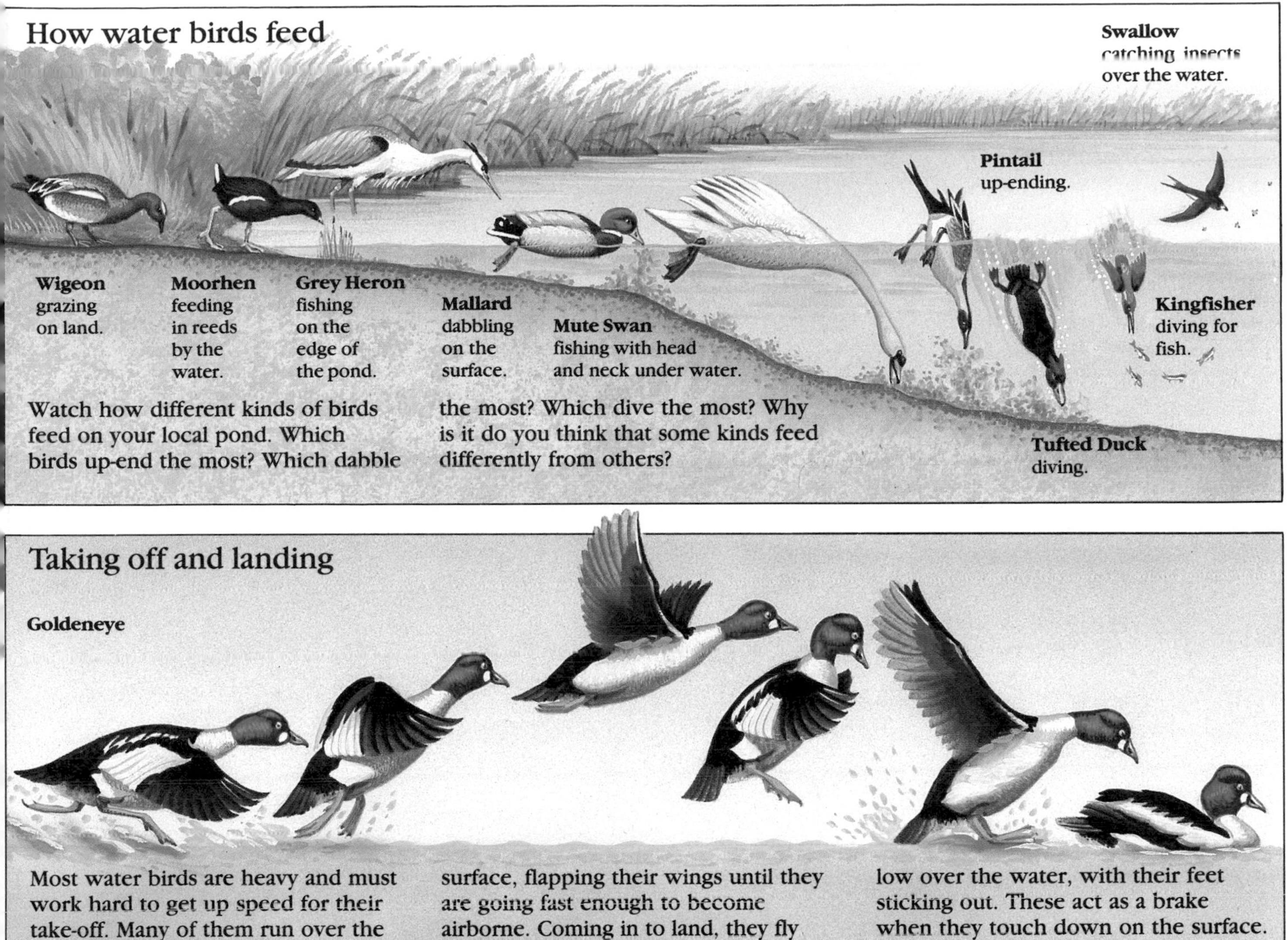

Watch how different kinds of birds feed on your local pond. Which birds up-end the most? Which dabble the most? Which dive the most? Why is it do you think that some kinds feed differently from others?

Taking off and landing

Most water birds are heavy and must work hard to get up speed for their take-off. Many of them run over the surface, flapping their wings until they are going fast enough to become airborne. Coming in to land, they fly low over the water, with their feet sticking out. These act as a brake when they touch down on the surface.

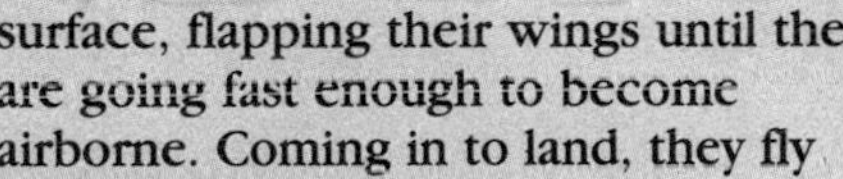

Gull

Moulting

Mallards moult in late summer. The male loses his colourful feathers and becomes a mottled brown all over. For a time he looks rather like the female. New bright-coloured feathers grow by early winter.

When danger threatens Mallard ducklings, the mother stretches out her neck and quacks loudly. The ducklings dive to escape.

Woodlands and forests

Woodlands and forests are good places to spot birds, but you will see them more easily in places that are not too dark. Woods with open spaces are lighter and have more plants and insects for birds to eat.

Woods with broad-leaved trees, such as oak and beech, contain many more birds than old pine forests, which can be very dark. But old pine forests can have special birds, such as Capercaillies, that can be found nowhere else.

The **Goldcrest** (9 cm) is the smallest European bird. It is often found in coniferous or mixed woods all year round.

The **Coal Tit** (11.5 cm) is the same size as a Blue Tit. It nests in coniferous forests.

The **Nightingale** (16.5 cm) can often be heard singing in woods and forests, but is rarely seen. It builds its nest among trees and bushes close to the ground.

The **Chaffinch** (15 cm) is a common bird, often found in broad-leaved woodlands and coniferous woods. In winter it prefers to live in open land.

The sizes given are beak-to-tail measurements.

The **Chiffchaff** (11 cm) is smaller than a sparrow and visits Europe from Africa during the summer. It is often found in broad-leaved woods and in young pine plantations.

If it is windy, watch out for falling branches in the woods. Try not to stand or sit near trees which have nests in them. You might frighten away the parent birds.

The food of woodland birds

The Tawny Owl feeds on small animals. Its eyesight and hearing are very good.

In autumn, Jays collect acorns. They bury many of them and then dig them up when they need food.

Many birds, such as the Garden Warbler here, feed on caterpillars.

The Pied Fly Catcher swoops down on insects from a look-out branch.

Jay

Special beaks

Some birds, such as the Hawfinch and the Crossbill, have special beaks for eating seeds.

The **Black Woodpecker** (46 cm) is the largest European woodpecker. It is found mainly in coniferous forests in many parts of Europe, but not in Britain.

Holes in trees

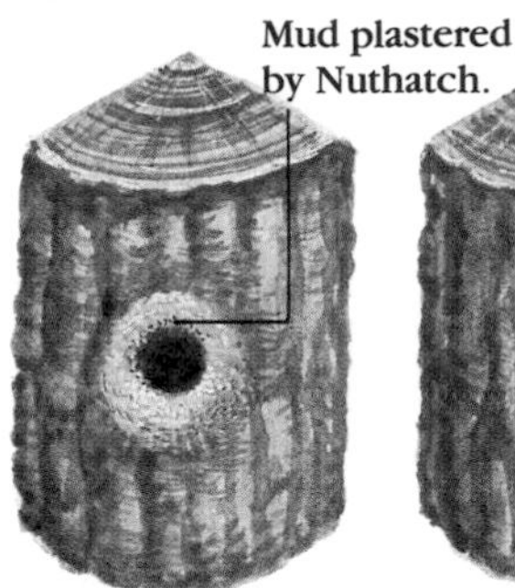

Hole used by a Nuthatch.

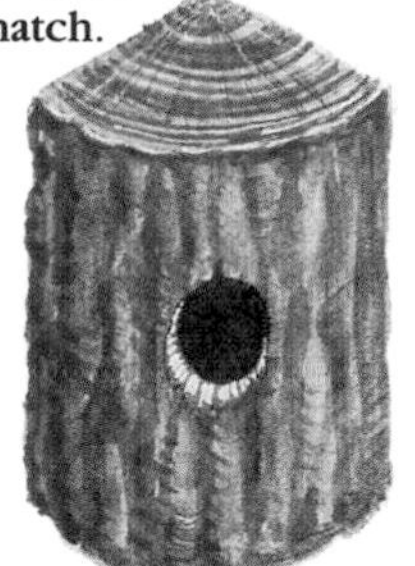

Hole used by a woodpecker.

Woodpecker holes

4 cm	4.5 cm	6.5 cm	10 cm
Lesser Spotted	Great Spotted	Green	Black

The different kinds of woodpecker all make nesting holes in trees. These are sometimes used by other birds, such as the Nuthatch, or even bats and dormice.

The **Nuthatch** (14 cm) feeds on nuts from hazel, beech and oak trees.

The **Green Woodpecker** (32 cm) is the same size as a pigeon. It is frequently seen on the ground, feeding on ants, and is usually found in broad-leaved woodlands.

The **Woodcock** (34 cm) is found in broad-leaved woodlands where its plumage blends in perfectly with the dead leaves on the ground. It has a long, thin beak.

The **Lesser Spotted Woodpecker** (14.5 cm) is the smallest European woodpecker. It is found in broad-leaved woods. The male bird has a bright red crown.

Woodlands at night

There are many different kinds of owl living in woods. They range in size from the small Pygmy Owl, which is only 16.5 cm high, to the much bigger Eagle Owl, which can be as large as 71 cm.

These three owls are all drawn to the same scale.

These four owls are all drawn to the same scale.

The Nightjar sleeps during the day, so is rarely seen. Its song can be heard after dark in summer.

Pygmy Owl **Scops Owl** **Little Owl**

Little Owl **Long-eared Owl** **Tawny Owl** **Eagle Owl**

Nightjar

Towns and cities

Bird spotting in towns and cities can be just as rewarding as in the countryside. In densely built up areas, you may only see Pigeons, Starlings and House Sparrows. Where there are gardens and parks you will find many other kinds of birds.

Some of these birds are quite used to people and can be very tame. You may even be able to get quite close to them and tempt them to feed from your hand. The pictures here show some of the most common birds in towns and cities.

The **Kestrel** is a town as well as a country bird. The town Kestrel usually feeds on sparrows, and nests high up on the tops of buildings.

Cliff birds that live in towns

Black Redstart

Black Redstarts once nested on sea-cliffs and rocks. Now you are more likely to find them in towns. They make their nests on buildings.

The **Long-tailed Tit** is a hedge bird that can often be seen in parks and gardens. In autumn and winter, family groups of about a dozen gather together.

The **Black-headed Gull** is one of the commonest town gulls. You will often see large numbers of them near reservoirs and gravel pits and in large grassy areas.

You will never see a **Swift** on the ground or on a wire. It feeds and even sleeps on the wing. At dusk, Swifts circle high above the roof-tops.

You will sometimes hear the warbling song of the **Skylark** as it flies above parks and wasteland. In winter, you may see flocks around gravel pits and reservoirs.

1

Towns and cities are surprisingly good places to look for birds. Birds need food and a place to rest and sleep. Most gardens (3) and parks (2) have

2

some trees and bushes where birds can nest and sleep without being disturbed by people. Many birds find perching places on buildings (5). Gulls fly out to

3

sleep at gravel pits (1) or reservoirs (4). Everywhere people spill or leave food which birds can eat. On the edge of town, birds find lots of food at sewage

Noisy city birds

The town Pigeon is a relation of the Rock Dove, which nests on sea-cliffs. The town Pigeon is now much more common than the Rock Dove and is often very tame. It feeds on bread and any other scraps it finds in parks or in the streets, and can be a nuisance in city centres.

Starlings are one of the most common city birds. They are usually found in huge, noisy flocks.

House Martins build their mud nests under the roofs of many town houses.

Carrion Crows are quite common in parks and gardens.

Magpies are large black and white birds and are common in parks and gardens. They use twigs to build their nests in tress and tall hedges.

Swallows look rather like House Martins, but have longer tail feathers. You can often see them catching flies over rivers, gravel pits and reservoirs.

works (4) and rubbish dumps (1). Railway sidings and canals (6), where food supplies are unloaded and often spilt, are also good feeding spots for birds, and have fewer people to disturb them. Many birds eat the seeds of weeds growing on waste ground and building sites. In winter, when there is little food in the countryside, many birds fly to the towns and cities. There many people put out food specially for the birds.

Sea coasts

The coast is always a good place to spot birds. In summer, many birds fly from Africa and the Antarctic to breed on European coasts. In winter, small wading birds, such as the Knot, come from the north to feed and wait for spring.

Most of the cliff-nesting birds spend the winter far out at sea. Every year many birds lose their eggs and babies because people tread on the nests or stop the parent birds from feeding the young by frightening them away.

Waders' beaks

Birds can find much food on the beach. The shape of a wading bird's beak depends on the sort of food it eats. You can try to find out what the birds are eating by digging up the sand and looking for the food in it.

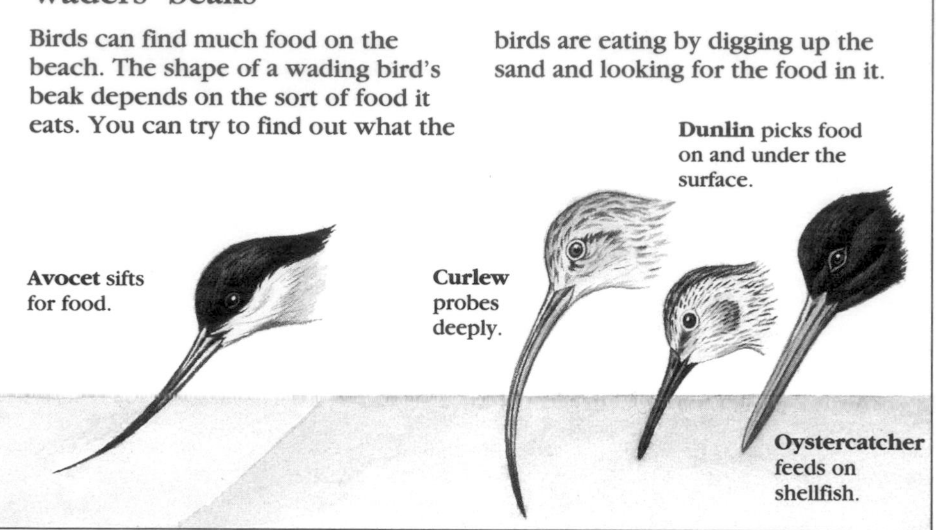

Nesting places

In winter, cliffs are almost deserted, but during the breeding season, they are like large bird cities. The whole cliff is used for nesting. Each type of bird has its favourite spot for nesting.

The **Brent Goose** is a rare winter visitor from Greenland and northern Russia where it breeds. It feeds on a plant called Eelgrass, which grows only on mudflats.

In winter, large flocks of **Knots** fly south from their northern breeding grounds. They feed on sandy or muddy shores. In winter, their plumage is grey.

The **Shelduck** is one of the most common large birds you will see on a salt marsh. Sometimes it builds its nest in an old rabbit burrow.

The **Common Tern** breeds on salt marshes, shingle or sandy shores. It builds its nest in a hollow in the ground.

Fish-eaters' beaks

Fish-eating birds do not all have the same kind of beak. The shape of the beak depends on the size and type of fish that the bird eats.

Gannets make their nests on cliff tops. Gannets nest in large numbers and build their untidy nests about one metre apart from each other.

Puffins use their bills for digging nesting burrows in the cliff top soil. They clear away the soil with their feet.

The **Fulmar** is a large bird that spends most of its time out at sea. It looks rather like a gull, but holds its wings straighter and stiffer when it is flying.

The **Razorbill** lays its one egg in a crack in the cliff or under a rock. The nest is sometimes a few pieces of seaweed, but often there is no proper nest at all.

The **Guillemot** makes no nest. It lays a single pear-shaped egg on a rock ledge. The shape of the egg stops it rolling off. They nest in large numbers.

The **Shag** is smaller than the Cormorant and does not have the Cormorant's white face. In the breeding season, it grows a little curly crest.

The **Cormorant's** feathers are not waterproof, so you will often see it standing on a rock or post holding out its wings to dry.

Moors and mountains

Many of the birds that live on moors and on mountains are well known because they are game-birds, such as Grouse. There are also large and powerful birds of prey, such as the Golden Eagle or Buzzard. You will see fewer birds in these places than at the coast or in woods because there is less food for them to eat. The smaller birds eat bilberries, young shoots of heather and seeds from mosses and grasses. The large birds of prey feed mainly on small birds and other animals.

The **Golden Eagle** is the largest bird that is found on moors and mountains. It is very rare in most parts of Europe.

The **Buzzard** is one of the most common of the large birds of prey. It is similar to the Golden Eagle, but is smaller and stubbier.

Every year people get lost on moors and mountains. Make sure it is not you. Never go on your own and always tell someone where you are going. Keep to paths and wear warm clothes.

The birds and mammals on these pages are not drawn to scale.

The **Short-eared Owl** nests on the ground. It often hunts in the daytime and feeds on small animals, such as voles and lemmings.

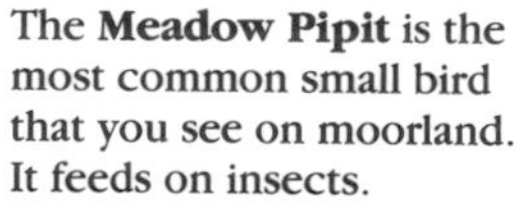

The **Meadow Pipit** is the most common small bird that you see on moorland. It feeds on insects.

These two birds look different, but are in fact very closely related. The **Red Grouse** is only found in Britain and the **Willow Grouse** only in Europe. The Willow Grouse is shown here in part of its winter plumage.

Red Grouse

Willow Grouse

Lemming

Changing colour with the seasons

The Ptarmigan can hide from its enemies because it always looks the same colour as the countryside. In summer, its coat is mainly brown. In winter it turns white. It lives in the mountains of northern Europe.

Shrikes

Shrikes (also known as Butcher Birds) have a habit of pinning insects, mice, lizards and even small birds onto branches or barbed wire. These food "stores" come in handy when fresh food is scarce. The Red-backed Shrike is a rare summer visitor. The Great Grey Shrike breeds in northern Europe and flies south in the winter. They can be seen in hedges, bushes, trees and on wires.

Red-backed Shrike

The **Raven** is the largest of the Crow family. It is as big as the Buzzard. The Raven flies slowly but powerfully, and sometimes tumbles through the air.

The **Black Grouse** lives on the borders of moorland. The male (blackcock) has curved tail feathers.

The **Golden Plover** usually breeds on moors and hills. It lays its four eggs in a nest on the ground.

The **Wheatear** builds its nest in holes in walls and in old rabbit burrows.

The **Dipper** lives by mountain streams. It feeds on insects it catches under water.

The **Ring Ouzel** is a relative of the Blackbird and lives in remote mountain valleys and on moors.

Migrating birds

Every year millions of birds move from one part of the world to another. This is called migration. Many birds come to Europe from southern Africa in April and May. During the southern African winter, which falls in June, July and August, there is not enough food for birds, such as Swallows.

Swallows fly north to breed in Europe where there is enough food. In late August and September they fly south where the summer is just starting. Again, the reason for this migration is to find good supplies of food.

Keep a record of migrant birds. Note down the first and last dates you see them. Also keep a record of the weather in spring and autumn. Does this have an affect on the dates when birds arrive or leave?

April 22nd
Weather warm and dry.
First swallows arrive from the south.

The Swallow

1 Swallows spend the winter months in southern Africa, but in March huge flocks start to move northwards to Europe. They come here to breed.

2 There is very little water in the desert, so the Swallows fly across it without stopping. They live off the food and water which they have stored as fat under their skin.

3 One of the most dangerous parts of the journey is crossing the Mediterranean Sea. Many Swallows take the shortest route, across the Straits of Gibraltar.

4 By the end of May most Swallows have arrived and built their nests. In late summer they get ready for the long journey back to southern Africa.

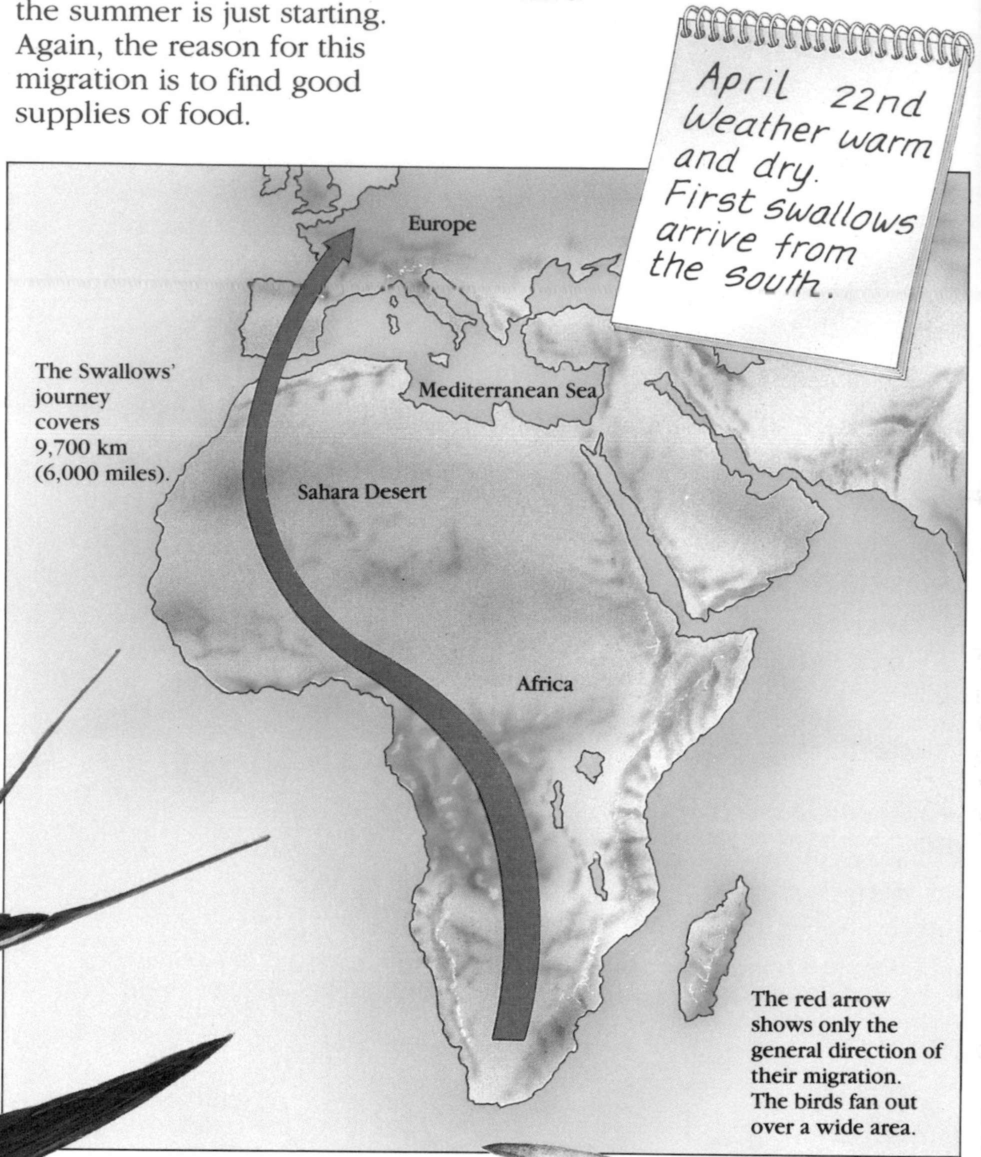

Europe

Mediterranean Sea

Sahara Desert

Africa

The Swallows' journey covers 9,700 km (6,000 miles).

The red arrow shows only the general direction of their migration. The birds fan out over a wide area.

Arctic

Arctic Tern

Some birds fly even longer distances than the Swallow. One of these is the Arctic Tern. It breeds in the Arctic and then flies south, all the way to the southern tip of South America and southern Africa. During the journey it stays mostly out at sea. These birds nest in large flocks, called terneries. The Arctic Tern shown here is in its summer colour. In autumn, the forehead is white and the bill and legs are blackish.

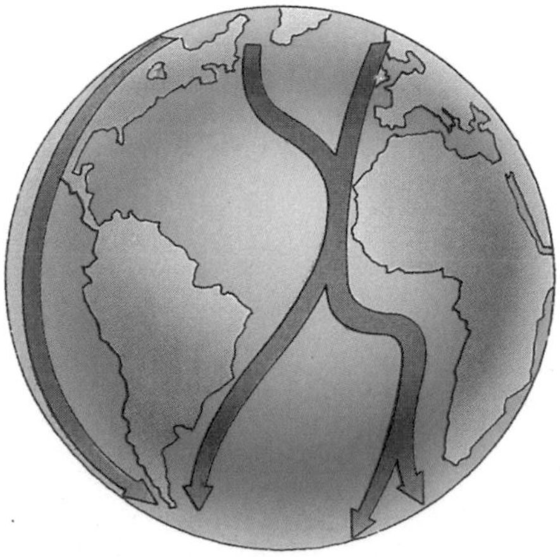

n some places in Europe, flocks of irds, such as White Storks, can be potted waiting by the coast for good veather, so they can continue their nigration across the sea.

The Redwing is a member of the Thrush family and looks like the Song Thrush but has pink on its sides. It is a winter visitor to Europe, coming from the north and travelling in large flocks.

The Hoopoe, with its parrot-like crest and floppy flight, does not seem capable of flying far, but every autumn it flies to Africa from Europe and makes a return journey in spring.

Summer visitors

The Blackcap and the Willow Warbler both belong to the warbler family and are two of the most common summer visitors to Europe. They come from Africa. In winter a few Blackcaps stay in Europe.

Many Starlings fly south in winter and are attracted to bright lights at night, such as lighthouses. Many of them are killed by flying into buildings where they see lights. Starlings are one of the most common birds in towns and cities.

Identifying birds by size

Sparrow-sized birds

The notes for each bird give size from beak to tail. Each panel has birds of a similar size. The dots beside each bird tell you where to look for it.

The birds inside this panel are all drawn to the same scale.

- Water
- Woods
- Towns and gardens
- Fields

Wren. 9 cm. Smallest bird you will see in gardens. Holds its tail cocked over its back.

Goldcrest. 9 cm. Smallest European bird. Feeds on insects and spiders.

Blue Tit. 11.5 cm. Only tit with blue head and wings. One of the most common garden birds.

Treecreeper. 12.5 cm. This mouse-like bird climbs trees.

Nuthatch. 14 cm. Has a sharp straight bill used for cracking open nuts.

Long-tailed Tit. 14 cm. Tail very long. Often seen in small flocks.

Great Tit. 14 cm. Has a black band down its belly.

Coal Tit. 11.5 cm. Has a white stripe on its neck.

Sand Martin. 12 cm. Has brown back and collar. Nests in holes in banks.

House Martin. 12.5 cm. Has a white rump and a shorter tail than the Swallow. Often nests in large flocks.

Swallow. 19 cm. Has long tail feathers and a dark throat. Feeds on insects.

Swift. 16.5 cm. Has very long curved wings.

Blackbird-sized birds

The birds inside this panel are all drawn to the same scale.

Starling. 21.5 cm. On the ground has an upright waddling walk. This common bird is often seen in large flocks.

Blackbird. 25 cm. The male is all black with an orange beak. The female and young are brown with a brown beak.

Song Thrush. 23 cm. Both sexes look the same, with a brown back and spotted breast. Often feeds on snails.

Mistle Thrush. 27 cm. A greyer bird than the Song Thrush and the spots on the breast are larger and closer together.

Remember - if you cannot see a picture of the bird you want to identify on these pages, turn to the page earlier in the book which shows birds that live in the place where you saw your bird.

Robin. 14 cm. Can be very tame. Has an orange breast.

Bullfinch. 14.5-16 cm. Has a black cap and white rump.

Greenfinch. 14.5 cm. Has yellow wing bars and a greenish rump.

Goldfinch. 12 cm. Has a red face and a black and white head.

Dunnock. 14.5 cm. Feeds on the ground and moves slowly with a kind of creeping walk.

House Sparrow. 14.5 cm. The male has a grey and brown head and black throat.

Tree Sparrow. 14 cm. Has a brown cap and a black spot on its white cheeks.

Chaffinch. 15 cm. Has white wing bars and white outer tail feathers.

Kingfisher. 16.5 cm. Catches small fish, shellfish and tadpoles for food.

The **Pied Wagtail** (18 cm) lives in Britain, the **White** (18 cm) in Europe.

Skylark. 18 cm. Has white outer tail feathers.

Yellowhammer. 16.5 cm. The male has a yellow head.

Linnet. 13.5 cm. The male has a red forehead and chest.

Great Spotted Woodpecker. 23 cm. Has large white wing patches and a black line from beak to neck.

Green Woodpecker. 32 cm. Has a bright red head and yellow rump. Often feeds on ants on the ground.

Cuckoo. 33 cm. Has a long tail. It lays its eggs in the nests of other birds.

Kestrel. 34 cm. The most common falcon. Often hovers before dropping on its prey.

Remember - if you cannot see a picture of the bird you want to identify on these pages, turn to the page earlier in the book which shows birds that live in the place where you saw your bird.

Crow-sized birds

The birds inside this panel are all drawn to scale.

Collared Dove. 32 cm. Has a black half collar at the back of the neck.

Woodpigeon. 41 cm. Has a white patch on each side of the neck.

Buzzard. 51-56 cm. Has broad wings and tail. Plumage is dark brown and cream.

Barn Owl. 34 cm. A large white-looking owl. It hunts in twilight or at night. The remains of meals can be found as pellets.

Lapwing. 30 cm. Has a thin crest and broad, black and white wings which show up when it is flying.

Herring Gull. 56-66 cm. Commonest gull on the coast. Has a large yellow beak with a red spot near the tip and grey wings.

Black-headed Gull. 35-38 cm. In winter, instead of a dark head, it has only a dark mark behind the eyes.

Mallard-sized birds

The birds inside this panel are all drawn to scale.

Coot. 38 cm. Larger than a Moorhen. Is all black with a white beak and forehead. Likes large open stretches of water.

Moorhen. 33 cm. Its beak is red and the underside of its tail white. Swims with a jerky movement.

Great Crested Grebe. 48 cm. The largest grebe. In summer, it has brownish frills round the neck. In winter, it has blackish ear tufts.

Tufted Duck. 43 cm. The most common diving duck. The male has a long drooping crest, the female is browner with a much smaller crest. They form large flocks on lakes and reservoirs.

Mallard. 58 cm. The male has a green head, white collar and purple-brown breast. Both birds have a blue patch and white bars on their wings, which show up best when they are flying.

Jackdaw. 33 cm. Has a grey head and is smaller than the all-black crows.

Magpie. 46 cm. A large bird with a long tail and black and white plumage.

The northern form of the **Carrion Crow** (47 cm) has some grey feathers. It is called the **Hooded Crow** (47 cm).

Rook. 46 cm. Has a thinner beak than the crow, with a bare white face and "baggy trousers".

Curlew. 51-58 cm. Largest wader. Has a long downward curved beak, a brown body and long legs.

Pheasant. Male 66-89 cm. Female 53-63 cm. A large gamebird. The male is brightly coloured, the female browner with a shorter tail.

Large water birds

Grey Heron. 90 cm. A large grey bird, often seen standing at the water's edge. The nest is usually built in a tree.

Cormorant. 90 cm. This sea bird has a white chin and cheeks. Often seen sitting on rocks with its wings half open.

Mute Swan. 152 cm. Has an orange bill with a black knob at the base. Swims with its neck curved.

Bewick's and Whooper Swan. 122 cm and 152 cm. Bewick's has a shorter bill with a small yellow patch. Both hold their necks stiffly when swimming. They are winter visitors.

INDEX

Books

The RSPB Guide to British Birds Holden & Sharrock (MacMillan)
A Field Guide to the Birds of Britain and Europe Peterson, Mountfort & Hollom (Collins)
Observer's Birds Hume (Penguin)
The Complete Book of British Birds (AA/RSPB)
The Bird Table Book in Colour Tony Soper (David & Charles)

Clubs and Societies

The national club for young birdwatchers is the Young Ornithologists' Club (YOC). Members receive their own magazine "Bird Life" every other month and may take part in competitions, projects and local outings. The club also organizes birdwatching holidays in many parts of Britain. The YOC is the junior section of the Royal Society for the Protection of Birds. Further details may be obtained from The Lodge, Sandy, Bedfordshire, SG19 2DL.

The British Trust for Ornithology organizes national surveys which are carried out by volunteers. It administers the ringing of birds. Junior members must be aged 15. Further details from Beech Grove, Tring, Hertfordshire IP24 2PU.

The Wildfowl and Wetlands Trust owns several reserves for wildfowl and carries out important research. For details about junior membership write to: Membership Secretary, The Wildfowl and Wetlands Trust, Slimbridge, Gloucestershire.

The Royal Society for Nature Conservation (22 The Green, Nettleham, Lincoln, Lincolnshire LN5 7JR) will give you the address of your local County Wildlife Trust, which may have a junior branch.

For a list of all local and national societies, look at the annual "Birdwatcher's Yearbook" by John Pemberton (Buckingham Press).